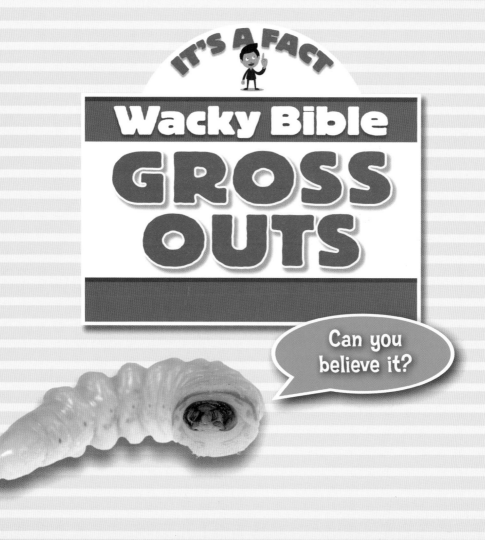

IT'S A FACT

Wacky Bible
GROSS OUTS

Can you believe it?

ZONDERKIDZ

Wacky Bible Gross Outs
Copyright © 2014 by ZonderKidz

Requests for information should be addressed to:

Zondervan, 3900 Sparks Ave, Grand Rapids, Michigan 49546

Library of Congress Cataloging-in-Publication Data

Wacky Bible gross outs : completely, 100%, historically accurate.
          pages cm. -- It's a fact
     ISBN 978-0-310-74424-5 softcover
     1. Bible stories, English--Juvenile literature. 2. Bible--
Biography--Juvenile literature. 3. Bible--Miscellanea--Juvenile
literature.
BS551.3.W26 2014
220.95'05--dc23   2013024685

Editor: Kim Childress
Contributors: Meghan Alexander, Kim Childress, Alyssa Helm,
Andrea Vinley Jewel, Kelly White
Cover and interior design: Kris Nelson/StoryLook Design

Printed in China

14 15 16 17 18 /DSC/ 18 17 16 15 14 13 12 11 10 9 8 7 6 5 4 3 2 1

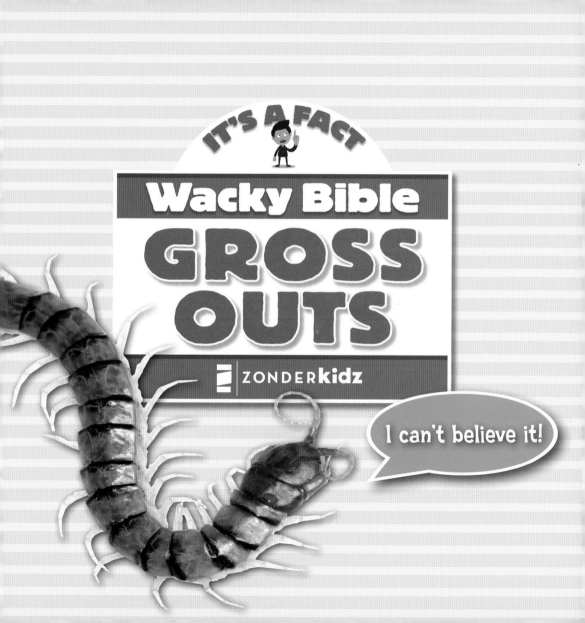

TABLE OF CONTENTS

Also in the series:

IT'S A FACT Wacky Bible Blockheads

section	title	page

section	title	page

section	title	page

Open your eyes to the SHOCKING, absurd, CREEPY, and downright stinky

stuff in the Bible that you never knew was in there.

The Bible is filled with **adventures, heroes, villains, feats of bravery, love, romance, monsters, angels, demons—** and some really **GROSS** and **DISGUSTING STUFF!** you would not believe!

Why does the Bible have so many gross things? Because life is messy. Because people do crazy things. Sin is not pretty.

Dig into *Gross-Outs* and astound your friends with these unbelievable facts. Maybe even get curious enough to explore more yourself—from the source.

Ribs aren't just for barbecues.

The first surgery
ever performed
happened when
God took Adam's rib
to create Eve.
God put Adam in a deep sleep,
took out a rib,
then closed the incision—
no stitches required.

Gathered to his people

When he was 175 years old, Abraham was gathered to his people. Gathered to his people is a Hebrew expression meaning Abraham joined his ancestors in death. Bodies were laid out on a rock shelf in a cave tomb. After the flesh had decomposed, or when the shelf was needed for another corpse, the bones were brushed to the back of the tomb, thus literally joining the ancestors.

That's unbelievable!

Adam lived **930** years.

Jared lived **962** years.

Methuselah lived **969** years.

15

God, um, can you please help me clean up this mess?

The Bible says effects of sin are as gross as a festering wound.

FESTER
means to
generate pus, putrefy, or rot.

A bandage won't cover that!

You are what you eat.

God cursed those who took Israel captive with wars, famine, and worse!

Famine means starvation.

They'd even eat their own children!

BUGS ANYONE?

When John was in the
WILDERNESS,
preaching about the coming of Christ,
he didn't have many food options.
CLAD IN CAMEL SKINS, you could
often find him munching on a
LOCUST.
MMM, TASTES LIKE CHICKEN!

MUD WRESTLING

David felt so stuck at times that he compared the feeling to being in a pit of

STICKY, SLIMY MUD.

Move one foot, the other slips
and sinks further. Try to crawl out,
get covered in more

MUD

and

SLIME.

The only way out was to

TRUST IN GOD.

THE DUMP

Jerusalem had a huge, open garbage dump just outside the city, in the Valley of Hinnom near Gehenna. In Gehenna, fire burned all day and night. **FLIES, MAGGOTS,** and all kinds of critters squirmed in and out of rotting food, **OOZING DEAD THINGS,** and **DUNG.**

The Gehenna Dump was so bad that Jesus used it to describe what hell was like—a place where "the worm does not die, and the fire is not quenched."

24

Nasty seven-year ditch

Nebuchadnezzar, king of Babylon, had become so proud God had to step in. He caused the king to lose his mind.

For seven years King Nebuchadnezzar went off to live with wild animals and became like one himself. He didn't shave, cut his hair, or trim his nails—for seven years!

Includes lots of disgusting facts involving blood.

The word

blood

is used

307

times in the
Old Testament

84

times in the
New Testament.

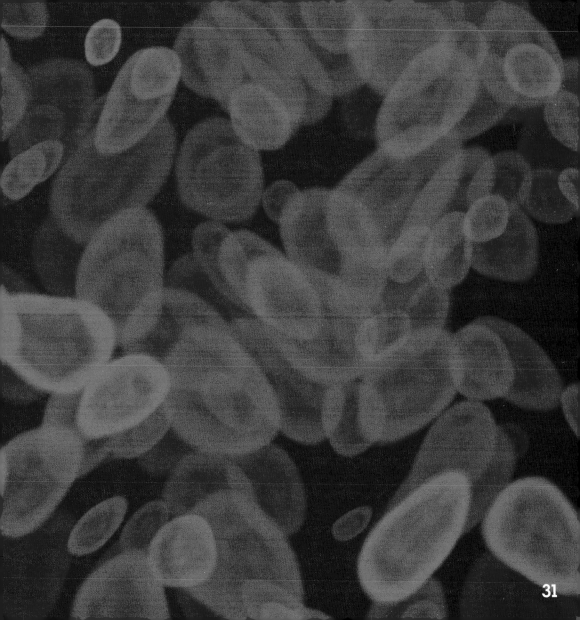

Cleansing Blood

Why did God require sacrifices?

Sacrifices were God's way of teaching SPIRITUAL TRUTH and HOLINESS to his people. God's holiness requires that sin not be ignored.

TO BE FORGIVEN OF YOUR SINS IN THE DAYS OF MOSES, YOU HAD TO SACRIFICE AN ANIMAL, AND A DIFFERENT ANIMAL DEPENDING ON THE CIRCUMSTANCE.

AFTER A SACRIFICE OF BULLS, MOSES PUT THE BLOOD INTO BOWLS AND SPRINKLED THE BLOOD ON THE PEOPLE— AS A SYMBOL OF BINDING THEM TO THEIR PROMISE TO FOLLOW GOD.

Animal sacrifices
were not taken lightly.
Before the animal was killed,
the priest placed
his hands
on the animal's head
in recognition of its
blood sacrifice.

WACKY PRIESTLY PRACTICES!

In Bible times it was believed that putting blood on the right **EAR LOBES, RIGHT THUMBS,** and **RIGHT BIG TOES** symbolically cleansed every part of a person's life.

THUMBS for the things they did.

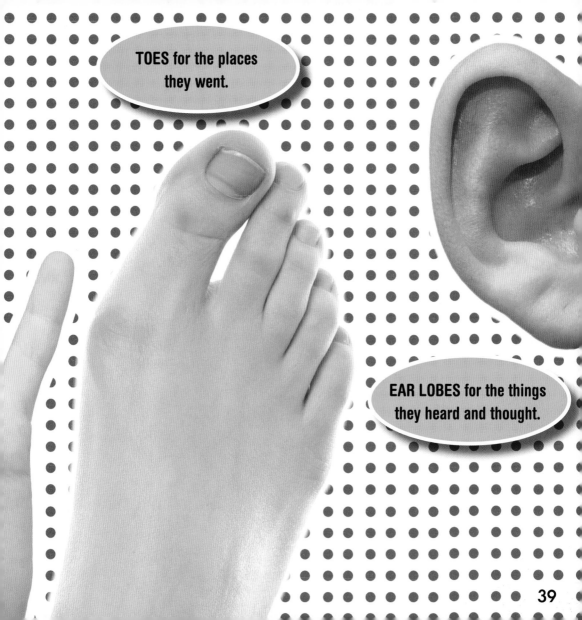

39

The Sin Offering

When priests dipped their fingers in the blood, God may have intended this gesture as a transfer of guilt. The blood of the sacrifice substituted for the blood of the sinner. The sacrifice died so the sinner could live.

Priests splashed blood on the sides of altars. This splashing of blood pointed back to the Israelites' exodus from Egypt, when the blood around doorframes indicated God's protection and deliverance. This also pointed forward to the shed blood of Jesus Christ, the Lamb of God, who paid the complete and ultimate price, once for all, for the redemption of humankind.

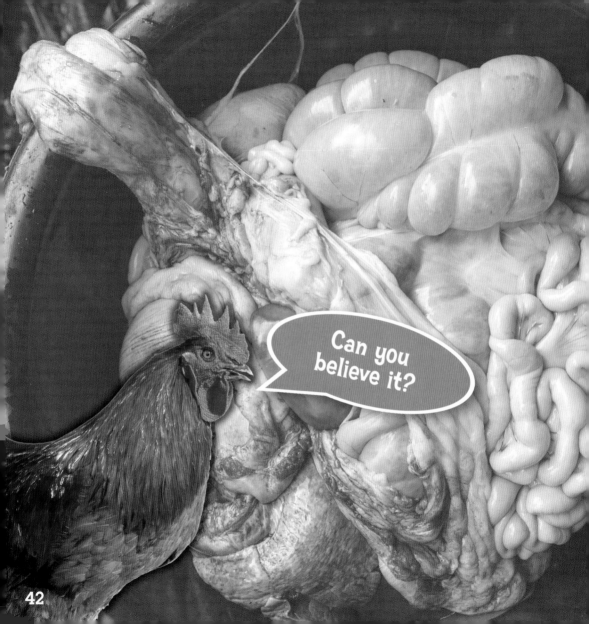

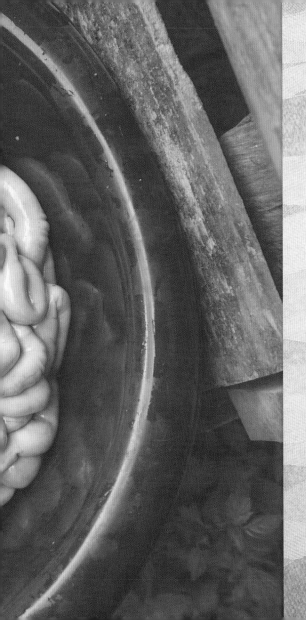

Some pagan sacrifices used animal organs for sorcery and predicting the future.

But the Lord commanded his people to burn the organs.

By commanding the organs be burned, the Lord was directing his people to not be like the pagans.

The giving and sacrificing
of animals was also a way people
made deals in Bible times.

With no police or lawyers, people
in Abraham's time would
cut the animal in half.

The two people making the deal
would walk between
the body parts.

Walking through the body parts
signified a covenant, an oath.

It was understood that a similar fate
should come on whoever
broke the contract.

In addition to the plagues God unleashed on Egypt in Moses' day, the Bible mentions plagues almost NINETY times.

Some were prophecies or warnings. Others were actual plagues that killed thousands of people.

49

What were some of the symptoms

of these different plagues?

Corroding flesh, eyes falling out of their sockets, and tongues rotting in the mouth, just to name a few.

GOD SENT TEN

#1 BLOOD

#2 FROGS

#3 GNATS

#4 FLIES

#5 DEATH OF LIVESTOCK

PLAGUES TO EGYPT

#6
BOILS

#7
HAIL

#8
LOCUSTS

#9
DARKNESS

#10
KILLING OF
FIRSTBORN

One dead fish smells bad. Imagine thousands. When God turned the Nile into blood, including

Blood

the streams, canals, ponds, and reservoirs, all the fish croaked.

Frogs

Frogs covered the land in the second plague on Egypt. **SLIMY, LOUD,** and **SQUISHY** frogs teemed in the Nile River and went up into all the homes, including the palace, all the bedrooms, on the people—even in the kneading troughs and ovens!

Everywhere the Egyptians walked, **CRUNCH, SQUISH, CRUNCH, SQUISH.** When Moses asked God to remove the plague, the frogs died wherever they happened to be—in houses, courtyards, and fields.

Plague Number 3:

Pharaoh's magicians called the third plague of gnats, "THE FINGER OF GOD." The Lord turned the dust throughout Egypt into gnats.

Gnats

Up until this plague, the magicians had kept pace with Moses' signs and wonders, but they could not replicate HORDES OF GNATS.

Imagine trying to sleep with gnats in your NOSE, your MOUTH, your HAIR …

DID IT STOP WITH THE GNATS?

NO!

Flies

Next came the fourth plague, flies throughout Egypt. Dense SWARMS poured into Pharaoh's PALACE and the HOUSES of his officials. But no flies were found in the land of Goshen, where God's people lived.

Plague Number 5:

During the fifth plague, God killed all the Egyptian ANIMALS IN THE FIELDS. When the Egyptians woke that morning, their ANIMALS WERE DEAD, while none of the Israelites' animals were harmed.

Death of Livestock

When God unleashed the sixth plague, festering boils broke out on all the Egyptians and their remaining

64

Boils

animals which had not been out in the fields. The magicians couldn't stand before Moses because of their boils.

Plague Number 7:

The seventh plague brought LOTS OF HAIL, which might sound somewhat enchanting. But have you ever seen baseball-sized hail? OUCH!

Plague Number 8:

The eighth plague involved locusts—think aggressive, **GIANT**, flying **GRASSHOPPERS**.

A locust swarm can number in the **MILLIONS** and devastate entire fields of crops in minutes. In Egypt, locusts **ATE EVERY PLANT** and crop in sight.

Locusts

Can you believe it?

Plague Number 9:

FOR THREE DAYS,

utter and complete

BLACKNESS

covered all of Egypt,

SO DARK

it could be felt.

Darkness

Plague Number 10:

After the darkness lifted came the death of

Death

firstborn sons.

GIVE US A PASS-OVER.

TO PROTECT THEMSELVES from God's tenth plague against the Egyptians, the Hebrews painted lamb's blood on their doorframes.

The Lord told Moses and Aaron, "The blood will be a sign on the houses where you are, and when I see the blood, I will pass over you. No destructive plague will touch you when I strike Egypt." (Exodus 11:4-5)

That month would become the FIRST MONTH of their year, and that day would become known as PASSOVER, when the Lord passed over the houses of the Israelites in Egypt and spared their homes when he struck down the Egyptians.

EVERYBODY POOPS!

What to do with the doo—and other bathroom Bible facts.

WHAT'S GOING ON?

After Jehu, king of Israel, demolished the temple of Baal, the Israelites **USED IT AS A PUBLIC URINAL** for hundreds of years. Since no one ever cleaned it in all that time, **CAN YOU IMAGINE THE SMELL?**

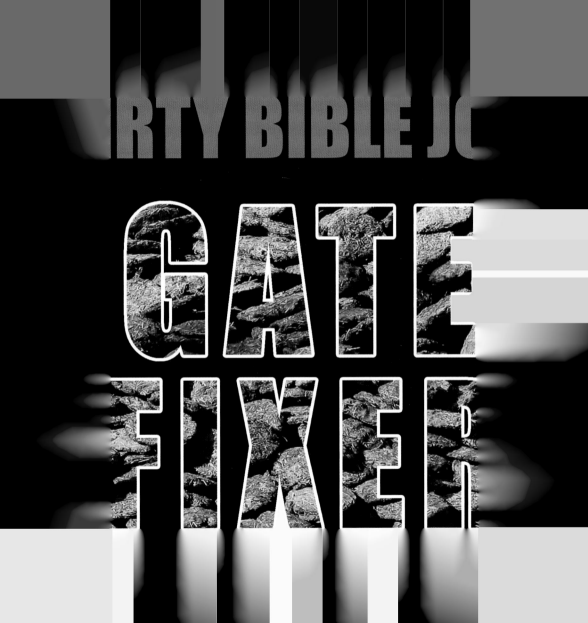

CAREERS

GENERAL HELP WANTED
Seeking someone for general help, eg; filing, organizing, errands, answering emails. Must know how to type. $10 per hour to start

★ ★ ★ ★ ★ ★ ★ ★

DIRTY BIBLE JOB:
GATE FIXER

Skilled worker needed to repair the Dung Gate, gate to the city dump, destroyed by fire. Must be able to rebuild and replace bolts and bars. Those sensitive to sickening stenches need not apply.

Call: 555-STINK

WEEKEND RECEPTION
We are seeking a general office assistant for Sund...

THE FIRST "OUTHOUSES"

Some of the Israelites had been going to the bathroom right inside the camp, where everyone could see and smell it.

GOD CAME TO THE RESCUE WITH SOME GOOD ADVICE:

1. Designate a place outside the camp where you can do your business.

2. Have a tool for digging.

3. Dig a hole, do your stuff, bury it.

"If you find honey, eat just enough–

too much
of it and
you will
vomit."

(Proverbs 25:16)

Don't eat
too much!

PIGS PREFER MUD BATHS

A proverb says, "A dog returns to its vomit," and "a sow that is washed returns to her wallowing in the mud."

This means, if a person believes in God and Jesus, he or she becomes free of sin. But if that person goes back to doing bad stuff, well, that's pretty foolish, like a butter-milk bathed, sparkling-clean pig returning to the mud.

JONAH DIDN'T MAKE A PRETTY LANDING ON THE BEACH.

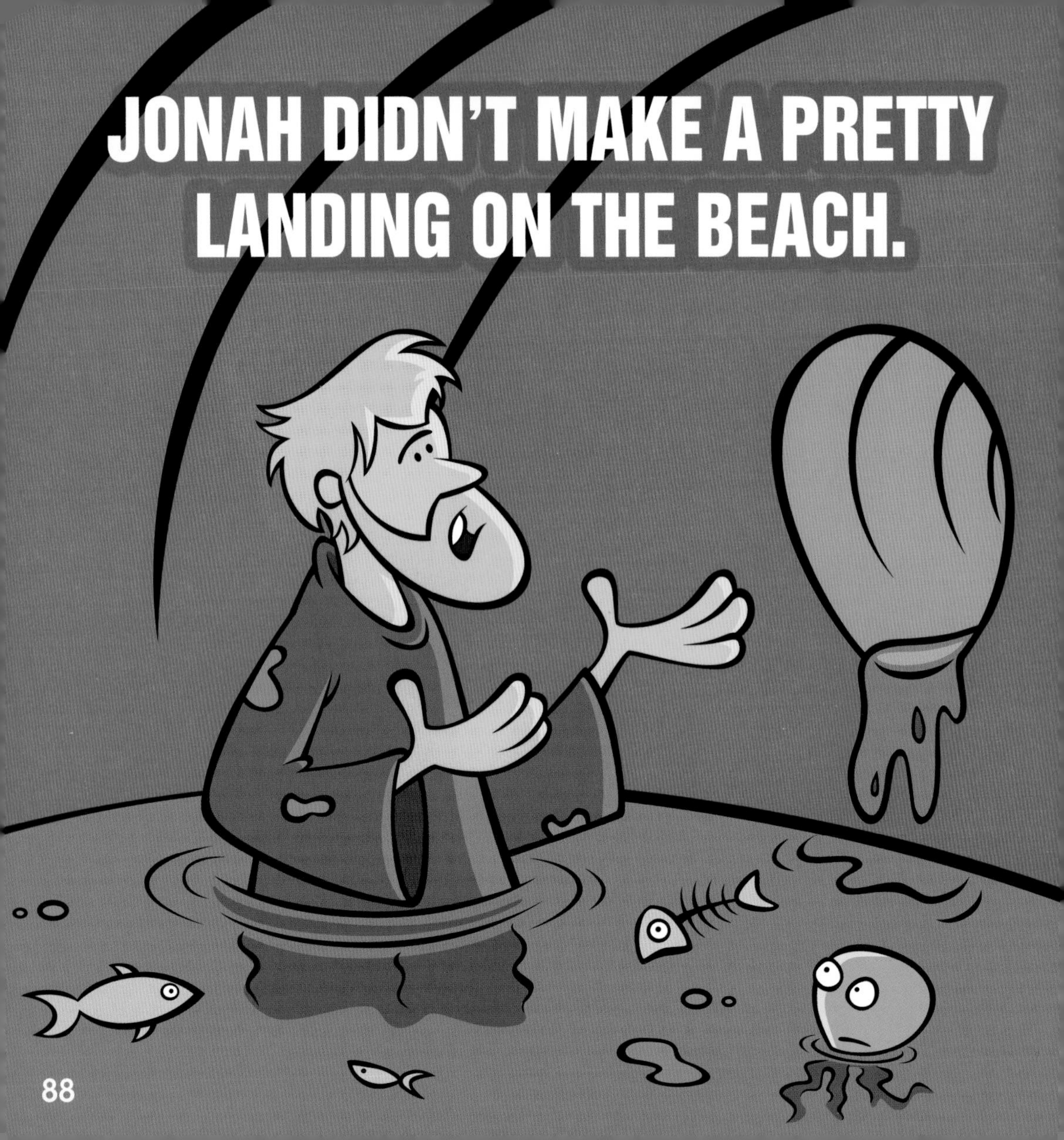

The whale spit him up—with everything else from its stomach, including

HALF-DIGESTED FOOD, SEAWEED, & STOMACH JUICES.

YUCK!

89

"You want me to do what?"

When Ezekiel was on the run from King Ahab and living in the wilderness, God told Ezekiel to cook his food over burning human excrement.

Ezekiel couldn't believe his ears. **HE PLEADED WITH GOD,** so God told him to use cow manure instead.

THE HEBREW WORD "madmenah" means "dunghill," and it was similar to the names of two Israelite towns, both called

MANMANNAH.

Some Bible scholars say these towns could have been

FERTILIZER PRODUCTION CENTERS.

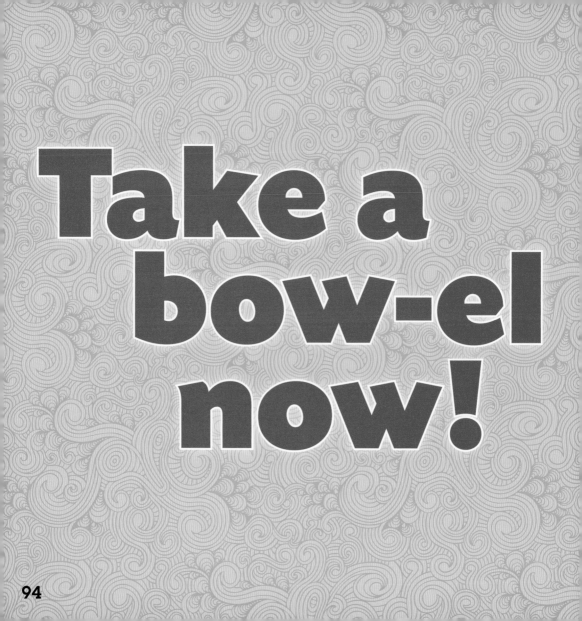

Take a
bow-el
now!

The prophet Elijah's prediction for Jehoram, king of Judah, was gruesome: Jehoram would get so sick to his stomach for so long that his bowels would eventually fall out of his body.

AND THEY DID!

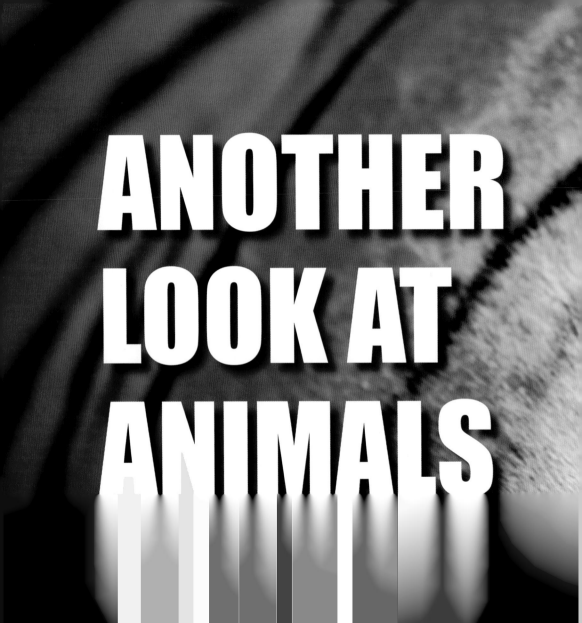

What to do with

ANCIENT ANIMAL DOO

Many Israelites were farmers with lots of animals. What do you think happened to all the scooped poop?

IT WAS PACKED AROUND FRUIT TREES.

Jesus told a story about a farmer fertilizing a fruitless fig tree growing in his vineyard.

IT WAS USED AS HAND CREAM.

Dung ended up in the dunghill, a.k.a. manure pile. God said the Moabites would "spread out their hands in it, as a swimmer spreads out his hands to swim."

IT WAS DRIED AND USED AS FUEL.

When Ezekiel was on the run from King Ahab and living in the wilderness, God told him to burn human poop to cook over. Ezekiel got grossed out, so God told him to cook his food over flaming cow manure instead.

Maggots, soft-bodied legless grubs, or worms, live off the dead.

Hell is compared to maggots eating rotting carcasses of flesh.

Get too close to a camel, and it might do more than spit on you.

When a camel feels threatened, it spews the contents of its stomach, along with saliva, to surprise or distract whatever or whoever is bothering it.

NOAH'S BOAT WAS LIKE ONE BIG ZOO ...

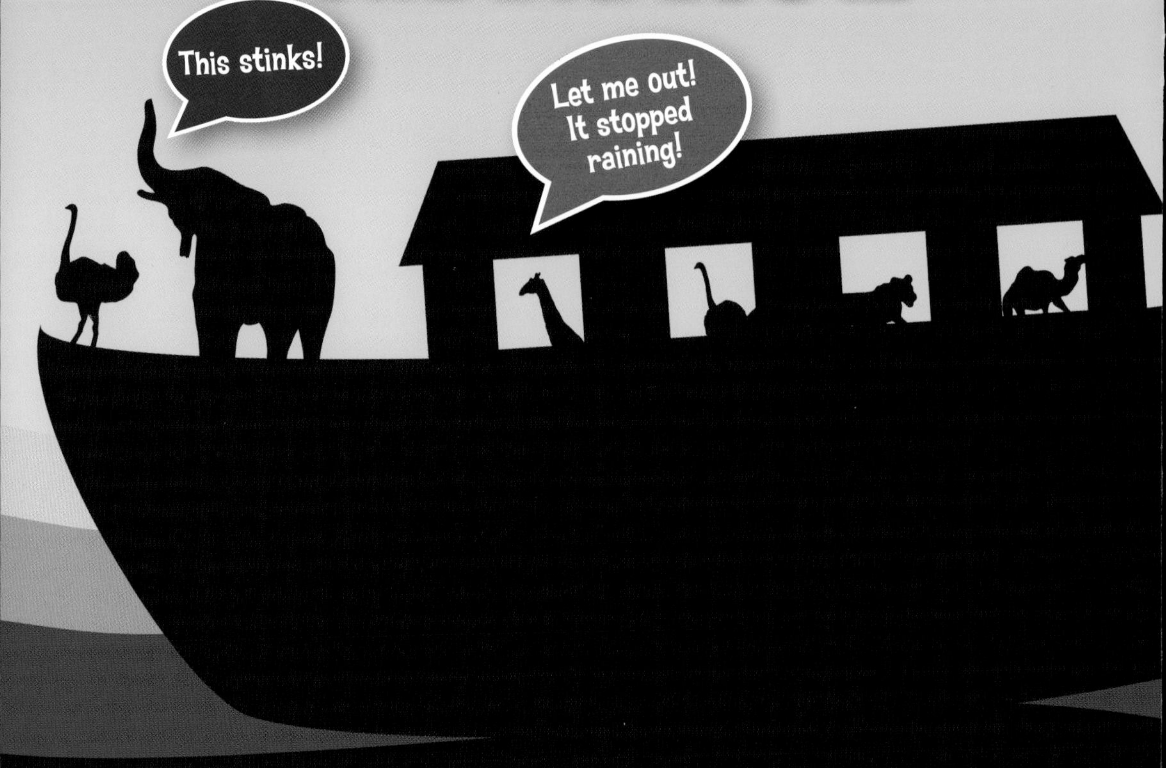

IN AN ENCLOSED SPACE, FOR OVER A YEAR. IT RAINED FOR FORTY DAYS AND FORTY NIGHTS, BUT IT TOOK A LONG TIME FOR THE WATER TO CLEAR.

NO PIT STOPS.
NO TRASH SERVICE.
NO CLEAN-UP CREWS—

EXCEPT FOR NOAH'S FAMILY. THAT'S A LOT OF WORK FOR EIGHT PEOPLE!

We have to wait for the water to go down!

GOD'S RECIPE FOR PURIFICATION

1. Burn a young cow.

2. Save the ashes.

3. Mix ashes with water. A gray, liquidy substance should appear.

4. Apply generously to help wash away sin.

That's what the Israelites used as a sin wash, but no amount of soap or scrubbing can fully clean up sin.

DURING
THE GREAT BATTLE

between the Israelites and the Philistines, Samson found a donkey's jawbone.

The jawbone was fresh, meaning the donkey hadn't been dead very long. So warm flesh probably still hung off it, full of bugs or picked over by birds. Samson grabbed it anyway and used it as a weapon.

Deep-Fried Donkey Skull

A whole head, delicately dirt-coated and flash-fried to perfection.

Bird Doo Brulee

Only the finest excrement ingredients, whipped to a deliciously not-too-sweet custard.

Famine in Samaria was so bad that people were eating donkeys' heads and using bird droppings as salt, fuel, or food—and those "grocery" items cost a lot of money!

Crocodile Lock!

Legend says the leviathan was a sea dragon with several heads. Most likely, leviathans were large crocodiles from the Nile River. Though a croc only has one head, it does have thirty teeth on each side of its jaw that lock into each other.

SUPER FLY!

Even one dead fly in perfume made the whole jar stink. The Israelites didn't have chemicals to preserve perfume, so one dead bug ruined the entire sweet aroma.

Beelzebub

One name for SATAN is BEELZEBUB, which can mean "lord of a fly," "lord of flies," or possibly "lord of dung."

STAMPEDE!

A herd of demon-possessed pigs ran off a cliff into a lake near Galilee that provided the water and food for the locals.

Soon the lake was polluted with

SMELLY,
BLOATED,
DEAD PIGS.

Evil uncovered is always ugly to see.

On the island of Patmos, John had a vision. FROGLIKE CREATURES came out of the mouth of a dragon. It's a sight that could MAKE YOUR EYES BLISTER!

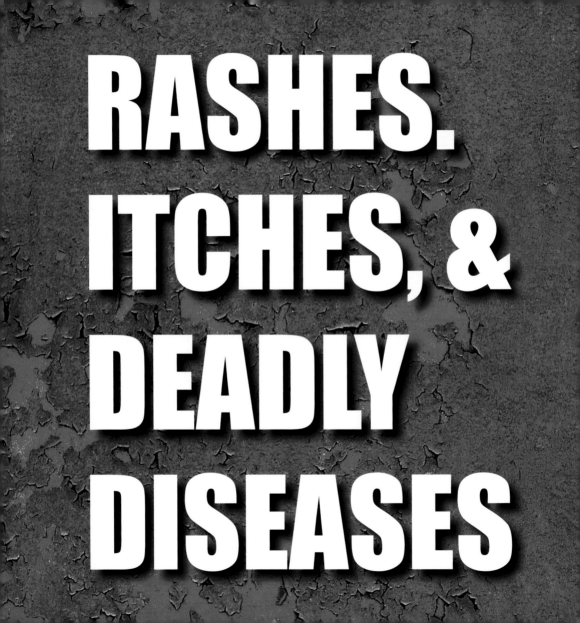

Top Ten Curses for Disobedience

There were drastic consequences for Israelites who disobeyed God:

1. **Wasting disease with fever and inflammation**

2. **Scorching heat and drought**

3. **Blight and mildew on your crops**

4. **Boils**

5. **Tumors**

6. **Festering sores**

7. **The itch from which you cannot be cured**

8. **Madness**

9. **Blindness**

10. **Confusion of the mind**

WHAT IS WASTING DISEASE?

Wasting Disease is a disease where a person "wastes" away, usually with CHRONIC FEVER and DIARRHEA. In Bible times, a person with wasting disease kept losing weight and fluids until he or she eventually died.

127

WHAT IS BLIGHT?

BLIGHT IS A DESTRUCTIVE DISEASE OF CROPS THAT **SPOILS** THE PLANT, PRODUCES **BROWN BLOTCHES** ON THE LEAVES AND FRUIT, UNTIL THE ENTIRE PLANT **WITHERS** WITHOUT ROTTING.

"What's your return policy?"

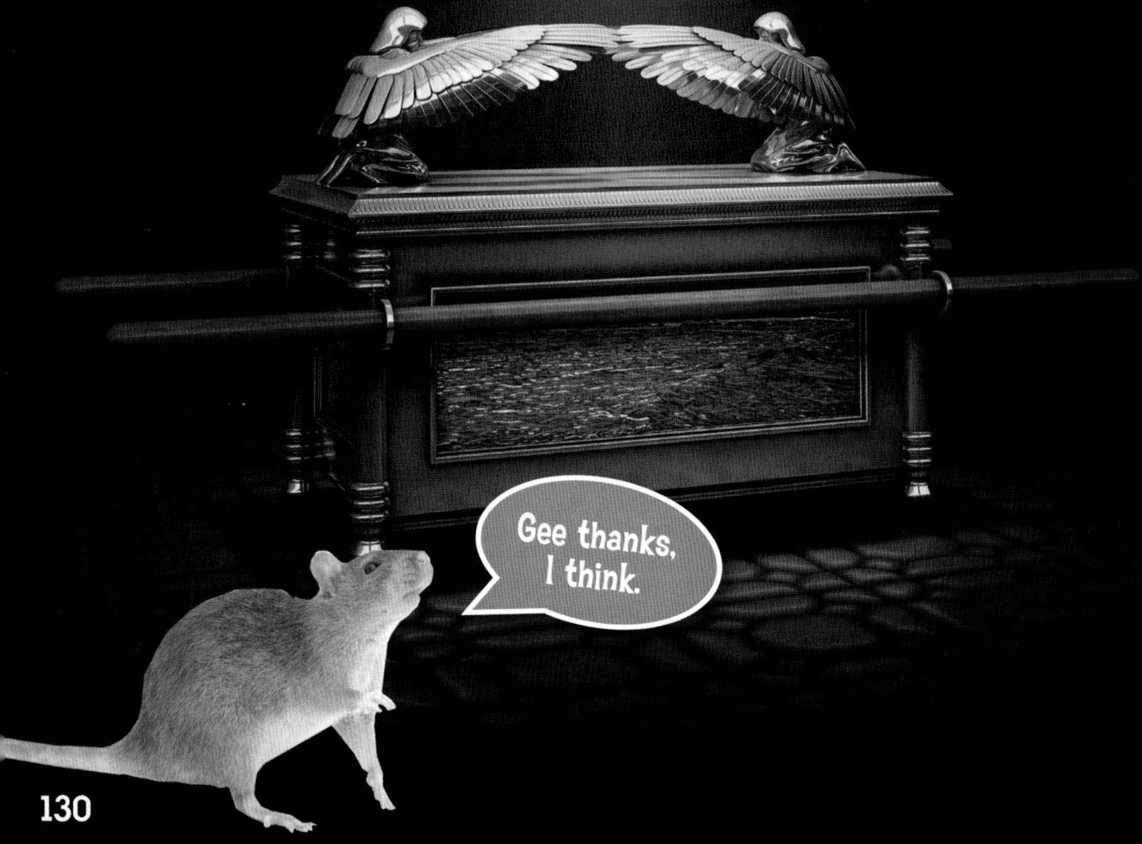

THE PHILISTINES QUICKLY LEARNED

that stealing the **ARK OF THE COVENANT** was a bad idea when they became infected with TUMORS, and **RATS** invaded their land. As a guilt offering, they sculpted **MODELS OF THE TUMORS** and **RATS FROM GOLD**, and they sent the models **BACK TO ISRAEL.**

JOB:

GOOD GUY
BAD LUCK

I can't believe it!

Job faced the worst diseases—
FOURTEEN OF THEM—including
BURNING ULCERS
and SKIN ROT.

When poor Job ended up covered with boils, he went out behind his house, took a piece of broken pottery and scraped his sores with it.

Some Bible experts say Job's boils were smallpox. Others think the boils were a parasite infection.

Job cried out, "My body is clothed with worms and scabs! My skin is broken and festering."

133

Gangrene is a disease that feeds on flesh. When blood flow stops to a certain part of the body, it kills tissues, muscle and fat, usually in toes and fingers, and can turn them black. Treatment? Usually amputation.

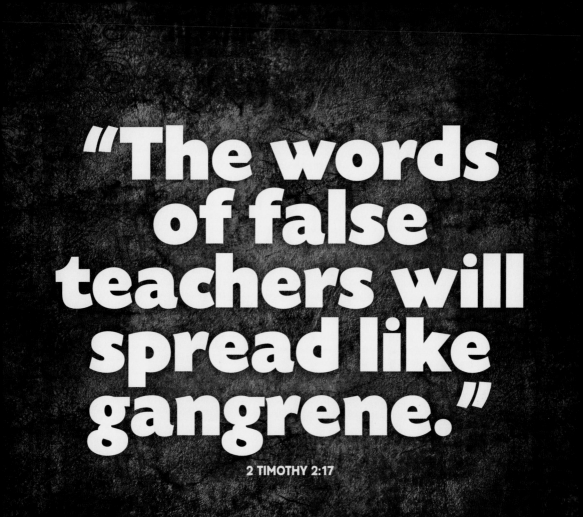

"The words of false teachers will spread like gangrene."

2 TIMOTHY 2:17

GRUESOME ENDS AND HORRIFIC PUNISHMENTS

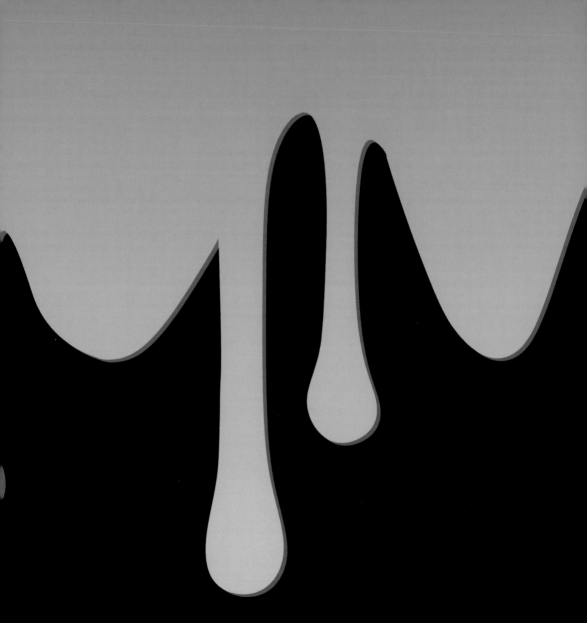

What a way to go!

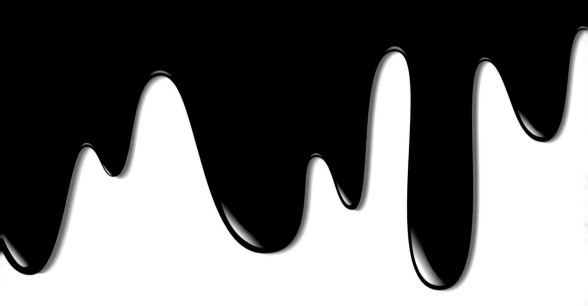

Tar pits were known as wells or fountains of SLIME, a GOOEY, ASPHALT-LIKE substance known as BITUMEN. The ancient Valley of Siddim was full of these TAR PITS, and when the kings of Sodom and Gomorrah went to battle, some of the men FELL INTO THE PITS and died.

MUMMIFIED!

Joseph asked the Egyptian physicians to embalm Jacob after he died. Egyptian embalming was so detailed it took forty days. It preserved each part of the body, even the eyebrows.

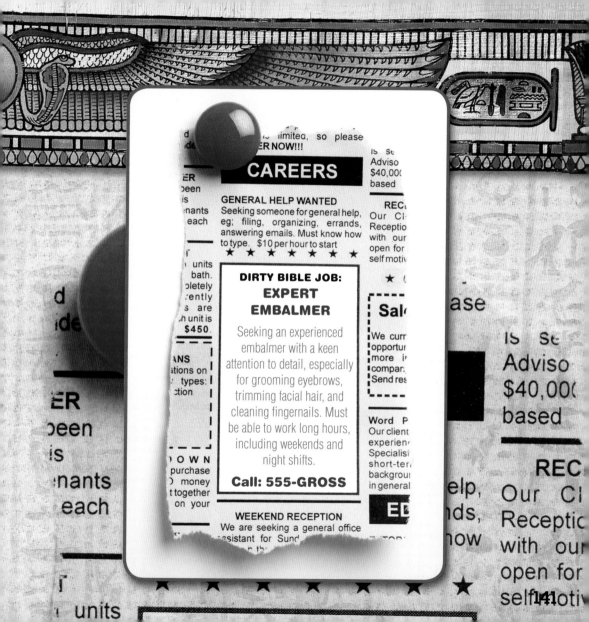

ON TV WHEN SOMEONE
IS **STABBED** WITH
A SWORD,

IT'S IN AND OUT,
A **NICE CLEAN CUT.**

Apparently, Joab's attack on Amasa wasn't so precise. His enemy's **SLIMY, SMELLY** intestines actually **POURED OUT.**

King Eglon of Moab was so large that when **Ehud stabbed him**, the sword got swallowed up by **Eglon's stomach.** Ehud couldn't get his sword out because the **king's belly fat** closed up around it.

WHAT A CRUEL PUNISHMENT: GOUGING OUT THE EYES.

Someone got up close enough to Samson to either scoop out his eyeballs, pierce them, or sear them with a red-hot iron.

THE DEATH OF KING SAUL

The Philistines split Saul's dead body in two. They fastened his head as a trophy on a wall in the temple of Dagon. Then they put his headless corpse on a wall in a nearby town.

Ishmael a cold-blooded assassin.

He slaughtered dozens of people. He dumped the dead bodies into a well to hide them.

In just a short time, Ishmael filled up the cistern with corpses.

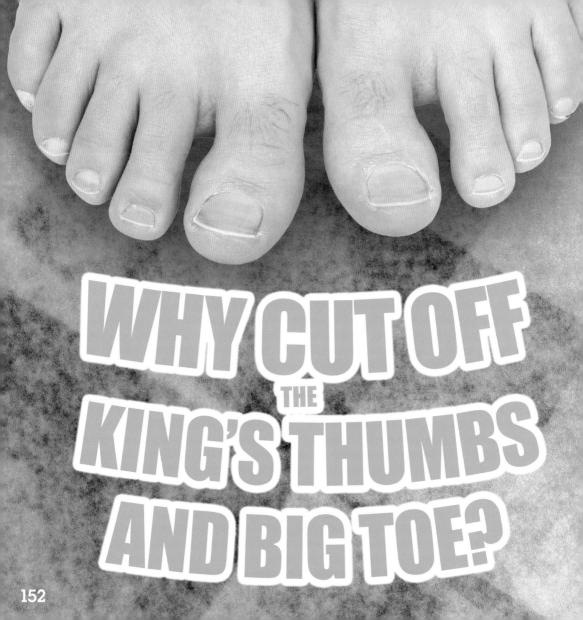

WHY CUT OFF THE KING'S THUMBS AND BIG TOE?

Judah's soldiers wanted to HUMILIATE and CRIPPLE the conqered king. Without THUMBS, he could no longer wield a weapon. Without BIG TOES, he could no longer run during battle. Such treatment of war prisoners was common among nations at the time.

BAASHA CAME TO BE KING OF ISRAEL BY MURDERING THE PREVIOUS KING, NADAB, AND THE ENTIRE HOUSE OF JEROBOAM (NADAB'S FATHER AND PREDECESSOR). BAASHA HAD PREVIOUSLY BEEN A CAPTAIN IN NADAB'S OWN ARMY.

THE CONSEQUENCE FOR THE EVIL WAYS OF BAASHA'S PEOPLE? THE DEAD WOULD BE LEFT IN THE STREETS AND FIELDS. NO ONE WOULD COME TO BURY THEM. SO DOGS AND BIRDS PICKED AWAY THE DEAD FLESH UNTIL THERE WAS NO MORE.

Several men had the **messy job** of recovering **dead bodies.** They looked in **caves, dens, ditches,** and among **thickets, thorns,** and **briers** for the carcasses and body remnants. They carried out the **bodies,** and then another group of men **buried the dead.**

It's a Party and You're Invited!

Where: King's Palace

When: Herod's Birthday

Dinner! Dancing!

Entertainment!

Please R.S.V.P.

When Herod's stepdaughter danced for Herod on his birthday, he promised her a gift in return,

anything she asked for, up to half his kingdom.

Her request?
The head of John the Baptist on a platter.

Lazarus

He was FOUR DAYS dead.

FOUR DAYS for body parts to start decaying. FOUR DAYS for the odors of PUTREFACTION to build. Nobody wanted to remove the stone of the tomb. THE STINK would have been overwhelming.

CONSEQUENCES FOR CHRISTIANS

Sometimes horrible things happened to Christians who didn't turn their backs on Jesus.

Some got sawn in two!

THE TRIALS OF PAUL

Jewish and Roman officials beat Paul with whips and rods at least eight times. Once he was stoned and left for dead. The sea even took its toll on Paul, shipwrecking him three times. His body was battered and bruised.

The soldiers
made a crown of thorns
and forced it onto Christ's
head. Then they hit him on the
head with a big stick. By the end
of the day, his face would have
been covered in blood from
the puncture wounds of the
thorns and the beatings.

Scripture Index

Sources

Baker, Anisa, ed., *801 Questions Kids Ask About God with Answers from the Bible.* Carol Stream: Tyndale House Publishers, 2000.

Lockyer, Herbert, *All the Men/All the Women of the Bible Compilation*. Grand Rapids: Zondervan, 2006.

Rasmussen, Carl G., *Zondervan Atlas of the Bible, Revised Edition*. Grand Rapids: Zondervan, 2010.

Strauss, Ed, *Seriously Sick Bible Stuff, 2:52 Series*. Grand Rapids: Zondervan, 2007.

Tenney, Merrill C., Silva, Mois's, editors, *The Zondervan Encyclopedia of the Bible, Revised Edition, Volume 5*. Grand Rapids: 2009.

Zondervan Publishing, *NIV Boys' Bible. New International Version*. Grand Rapids: Zondervan, 2012.

Zondervan Publishing, *NIV Quest Study Bible*. New International Version. Grand Rapids: Zondervan, 2011.

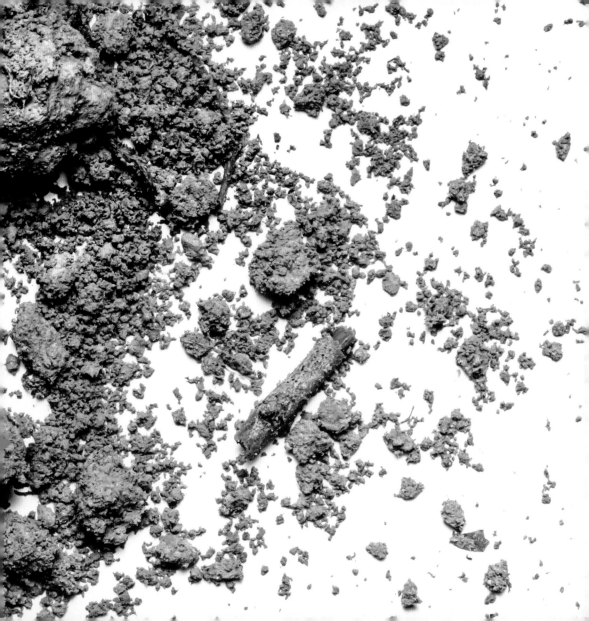

NOT EVERYONE IN THE BIBLE WAS AS WISE AS KING SOLOMON.

YOU'D THINK SAMSON WOULD HAVE FIGURED OUT HIS WIFE WAS OUT TO GET HIM AFTER THE FIRST TWO ATTEMPTS ON HIS LIFE.

WHEN GOD SAYS, "DON'T LOOK," LOT'S WIFE MAKES A PRETTY GOOD EXAMPLE OF WHY YOU SHOULD LISTEN.

EVEN DAVID, A "MAN AFTER GOD'S OWN HEART," MADE SOME PRETTY "BLOCKHEAD" MOVES.

From the **IT'S A FACT** series, *Wacky Bible Bible Blockheads* highlights "duh" moments in the Old and New Testaments some you may know, others that may surprise. Astound your friends and maybe even inspire someone to pick up the Bible and explore these facts for themselves.

We want to hear from you. Please send your comments about this book to us in care of zreview@zondervan.com. thank you.